Expository Nuggets
from the
Gospels

Expository Nuggets
from the
Gospels

Stuart Briscoe Expository Outlines

D. Stuart Briscoe

A Division of Baker Book House Co
Grand Rapids, Michigan 49516

© 1994 by D. Stuart Briscoe

Published by Baker Books
a division of Baker Book House Company
P.O. Box 6287, Grand Rapids, MI 49516-6287

ISBN: 0-8010-1063-2

Second printing, December 1994

Printed in the United States of America

Contents

Part 2: Discipleship

Part 3: How Jesus Explained It

Part 4: The Difference Christ Makes Today

Part 5: Getting Ready for Christmas

Preface

Outlines and skeletons are quite similar. Sermons without outlines tend to "flop around" like bodies without bones. But bones without flesh are not particularly attractive; neither are outlines without development. The outlines presented in this book are nothing more than skeletal for a very good reason. I have no desire to produce ready-made sermons for pastors who need to develop their own, but on the other hand I recognize that many busy pastors who find sermon-preparation time hard to come by may at least use them as a foundation for their own study, meditation, and preaching. They can add flesh to the bones; they can add development to structure. All the sermons based on these outlines have been preached during the last twenty-two years of my ministry at Elmbrook Church in Milwaukee, Wisconsin, and as one might expect, they vary in style and substance—not to mention quality! I trust, however, that they all seek to teach the Word and apply it to the culture to which they were preached, and if they help another generation of preachers as they "preach the Word," I will be grateful.

Part 1

Knowing How to Behave— The Sermon on the Mount

1

Behavior

Matthew 5:1-2

After "knowing what to believe" we need "knowing how to behave." The Sermon on the Mount will be the basis of our study.

I. The dynamics of human behavior
   A. Motivational forces produce individual drives
     1. Self-preservation
     2. Self-gratification
     3. Self-glorification
   B. Moral factors produce social awareness
     1. Conscience that is in-built
     2. Community thinking that is imposed
     3. Convictions that are introduced
   C. Mechanism of choice produces balance between motivational and moral factors
     1. Ability to discern
     2. Ability to discriminate
     3. Ability to decide

II. The difficulties of human behavior
   A. Its causes
      1. Unrestrained motivational forces
      2. Unsatisfactory moral factors–for example, too weak or too strong
      3. Unheeded mechanical failures
         Note: Problem of fallen humanity (Rom. 7:15–25)
   B. Its consequences
      1. Individual confusion
      2. Social corruption

III. The distinctives of Christian behavior
   A. A matter of morality–mountain revelation not human speculation
   B. A matter of mentality–learning by exposition not experimentation
   C. A matter of mastery–discipleship not ego trip
   D. A matter of minority–the multitude is usually wrong

2
Happiness Is...

Matthew 5:3-5

The message of Christ starts with happiness (blessedness), for God is a "blessed God" (1 Tim. 1:11). There are hindrances to happiness—sinfulness and selfishness—and therefore he deals with these. But happiness is what he wants for us.

Note: Blessed (Gk., *makarios*) in secular Greek described the state of the gods. It means "contented, fulfilled, to be congratulated."

I. Happiness is the product of character
   A. A realistic character—"poor in spirit"
     (Matt. 5:3)
     1. Realistic about spiritual inability
       a. John 3:3
       b. John 7:34
       c. John 15:4
       d. Romans 8:8
       e. 1 Corinthians 2:14

  2. Realistic about spiritual inadequacy
   a. Genesis 32:10
   b. Judges 6:15
   c. Isaiah 6:5
 B. A repentant character—"they that mourn"
  (Matt. 5:4)
  1. Consciousness of general conditions
  2. Confession of personal condition
   a. Psalm 51:3
   b. Job 42:6
   c. Luke 5:8
 C. A responsive character—"the meek" (Matt. 5:5)
  1. Meekness is not weakness
  2. Meekness is response to God in adoration
  3. Meekness hates reaction against God in
   antagonism

II. Happiness is the promise of Christ
 A. The authority of his statements
 B. The availability of his blessings
  1. Spiritual riches for poverty
  2. Spiritual comfort for sorrow
  3. Spiritual triumph for surrender
 C. The acceptance of his provision

3

Happiness Is Also...

Matthew 5:6-8

I. Happiness is the product of character
  A. Ambition based on "right" (v. 6)
     Note: "hunger and thirst"
     1. Ambition is normal
     2. Ambition may be perverted
        a. Power hungry (Isa. 14:12–15)
        b. Fun hungry (Luke 12:19)
        c. Fame hungry (Dan. 4:30)
     3. Ambition must be directed
        a. To possessing righteousness (Phil. 3:9)
        b. To practicing righteousness (Phil. 1:11)
        c. To promoting righteousness (Prov. 14:3)
           (1) Not what is easiest
           (2) Not what is expedient
           (3) Not what is profitable

   B. Attitude based on "kindness" (Matt. 5:7)
      Note: *merciful*–literally, "kind"
      1. God is rich in mercy (Eph. 2:4)
      2. God is ready to be merciful (Exod. 34:6)
      3. God reproduces merciful people (Phil. 2:1)
         a. Because they enjoy the mercy of God
         b. Because they understand the needs of people
      4. God requires a merciful attitude
   C. Action based on "truth" (Matt. 5:8)
      Note: *pure*–literally, "free from alloy"
      1. Action springs from motivation
      2. Motivation may be insincere (Acts 5:1–4)
      3. Action must spring from truth because
         a. God examines motives (Ps. 139:23–24)
         b. God exposes hypocrisy (Acts 8:19–23)
         c. God expects reality (Ps. 51:6)

II. Happiness is the promise of Christ (Matt. 5:6–8)
   A. The promise of spiritual fullness–"shall be filled"
   B. The promise of natural kindness–"shall obtain mercy"
   C. The promise of eternal joyfulness–"shall see God"

4

Happiness Is Furthermore...

Matthew 5:9-12

Happiness is the product of character and the promise of Christ. Here are some more Christian characteristics and promises.

I. Character that pursues peace (v. 9)
   A. The passion for peace
      1. A passion for spiritual peace (2 Cor. 5:20)
      2. A passion for social peace (Rom. 12:18)
      3. A passion for personal peace (Matt. 5:24)
   B. The price of peace
      1. Blood must be spilled (Col. 1:20)
      2. Barriers must be broken
      3. Bridges must be built
   C. The pursuit of peace (1 Peter 3:11; Rom. 14)
      1. Principles must be clear (no peace with evil or error)
      2. Power must be claimed (Gal. 5:22–23)
      3. Performance must be commenced

D. The prize of peace
  1. Blessing of God
  2. Recognition as children of God

II. Character that persists under persecution
  (Matt. 5:10–12)
  Note: "not peace but a sword" (Matt. 10:34)
  A. Persecution should be expected–identification
     with . . .
     1. Christ is alienation from Satan
     2. Right is alienation from sin
     3. Truth is alienation from lies
  B. Persecution may be expensive
     1. Physical persecution
     2. Character assassination
     3. Social ostracism
  C. Persecution can be excellent
     1. It confirms the believer (1 Peter 4:12)
     2. It confers the blessing

5

Salt of the Earth

Matthew 5:13

Having outlined the principles and qualities of distinctive Christians and their behavior, the Lord goes on to explain the importance and impact of this behavior in society. He compares it to salt.

I. The status of "being salt"
   A. Christ regards them as being salt
      Note: "ye are"
   B. World requires them to be salt
      1. Because salt is imperative for survival
      2. Because salt is distinctive in nature
      3. Because salt is abrasive in character

II. The significance of "being salt"
   A. As a means of arresting corruption
      Note: fisherman's use of salt (1 Cor. 1:18)
   B. As a means of attesting covenants (Num. 18:19; see 2 Cor. 3:6)

    C. As a means of affirming condemnation (Judg.
       9:45; see 2 Cor. 2:16; 1 Kings 18:17–18; Acts
       7:54–60)
    D. As a means of administering cleansing (Ezek.
       16:4; see Acts 19:18–20; Neh. 13:23–31)
    E. As a means of adding content (Job 6:6)

III. The seriousness of "being salt"
    A. Possible danger (see Rom. 1:22)
       Note: "lose savor" (Gk. *mōrainō*)
       1. Social conformity
       2. Spiritual complacency
       3. Moral confusion
    B. Possible disgrace
       1. Lost uniqueness
       2. Lost usefulness
    C. Possible disaster
       1. Society's rejection of saltless saints

6

Light of the World

Matthew 5:14-16

Distinctive Christian behavior not only acts as salt on earth but also functions as light in the world.

I. An explanation (v. 14)
   A. A continuation ministry
      1. "I am the light of the world" (John 9:5)
      2. "You are the light of the world" (Matt. 5:14)
   B. A clarification ministry
      1. Exposing the dangers of darkness (John 8:12)
      2. Explaining the light of life (John 8:12)
   C. A coordination ministry
      1. God created *kosmos* (world)
      2. Man created *chaos*
      3. Light on kosmos brings order to chaos
   D. A consolidation ministry (Matt. 5:14)
      1. An inflexible point of reference
      2. An impregnable place of refuge

II. An expectation (v. 15)
   A. That obstacles will be avoided—"bushel"
      1. Bushel of indifference
      2. Bushel of inconsistency
   B. That opportunities will be accepted
      1. The strategic position of candlestick
      2. The prolific light from candlestick
   C. That obligations will be acknowledged

III. An exhortation (v. 16)
   A. Method of shining
      1. Works that are viable
      2. Works that are visible
   B. Means of shining
      1. Kindle the flame
      2. Remove the bushel
      3. Trim the wick
      4. Replenish the oil
   C. Motivation for shining
      1. The glory of God
      2. The blessing of mankind

7

God's Moral Law

Matthew 5:17-20

The biblical teaching of God's absolute moral standards has fallen on hard times. The results are easy to see. A clear restatement is necessary.

I. The importance of the moral law
   A. Enacted by God (Exod. 20:1-7)
      1. A revelation of his being
         a. Lord
         b. God
         c. Thine
         d. Relevant
      2. His requirements for behavior
         a. Godward (vv. 4-11)
         b. Manward (vv. 12-17)
   B. Enforced by prophets
      1. Moses (Deut. 30:11-20)
         a. Command (v. 16)
         b. Choice (v. 19)

      2. Isaiah (Isa. 1:18–20)
         a. Obedience (v. 19)
         b. Disobedience (v. 20)
      3. Malachi (Mal. 3:7–15)
         a. Return (v. 7)
         b. Reject (vv. 14–15)
  C. Endorsed by Christ (Matt. 5:17)
      1. Affirmed by his life (John 8:29)
      2. Amplified by his teaching (Matt. 7:12; Matt. 22:40)
      3. Acknowledged by his death (Gal. 3:13)
      4. Answered by his Spirit (Rom. 8:4)

II. The permanence of the moral law (Matt. 5:18)
  A. An authoritative statement–"verily I say"
  B. An absolute standard–"jot or tittle"
  C. An assured stability (Matt. 7:24)

III. The relevance of the moral law (Matt. 5:19–20)
  A. As a principle of Christian behavior (v. 19)
      1. Disobedience plus denial equals disgrace
      2. Doing plus disseminating equals distinction
  B. As a prelude to Christian conversion (v. 20)
      1. By rejecting self-righteousness (e.g., scribes and Pharisees)
         a. Adherence to the letter
         b. Avoidance of the spirit
      2. By revealing unrighteousness (see Gal. 3:10)
      3. By requiring God's righteousness (Phil. 3:9)
         a. Imputed
         b. Imparted

8

Anger and the Christian

Matthew 5:21-26

Having stated his position concerning the importance, permanence, and relevance of the moral law, the Lord begins to deal with specifics.

I. Some basic assumptions (v. 21)
  A. He assumes knowledge of the law
    1. Taught in private (Deut. 6:6–9)
    2. Read in public (Neh. 8:8)
  B. He assumes respect for the law
    1. Because of its source (Exod. 20:1–2)
    2. Because of its scope (Exod. 20:3–17)
    3. Because of its severity (Exod. 21:12–17)

II. Some bold assertions (Matt. 5:22)
  A. Concerning equivalents
    1. His words and law merit equivalent attention, "But I say" (see also Matt. 7:29; Acts 17:31)

  2. Anger and killing merit equivalent
    punishment
    a. Judgment
    b. Council
    c. Hell fire
     (1) Because anger is murder's root (Gen.
      4:1–8)
     (2) Because anger kills personhood
      (a) *Raca*
      (b) More
     (3) Because anger destroys brotherhood
      (see Rom. 13:8–10)
 B. Concerning exceptions
  1. Killing may not be sin
    a. Capital punishment (Exod. 21:12–17)
    b. War (Exod. 23:20–24)
  2. Anger may not be sin
    a. Because it is evidence of love (see Eph.
     4:26; Neh. 5:1–8; Mark 3:1–5)

III. Some big actions (Matt. 5:23–25)
 A. Recognition
  1. Of anger's causes
    a. Mark 7:21–23
    b. Luke 15:28–30
    c. 1 John 3:15
  2. Of anger's characteristics (Eph. 4:31)
  3. Of anger's consequences (see Eph. 4)
 B. Rejection (see Col. 3:8–9)
 C. Reconciliation
  1. A prelude to worship (v. 24)
  2. A principle of life (v. 25)

9

Sex and the Christian

Matthew 5:27-30

I. Biblical teachings on sex
   A. Sex–the fact of life
      1. Sexuality a divine creation (Gen. 1:27)
      2. Sex activity a divine command (Gen. 1)
      3. Sexual unity a divine concern (Gen. 2)
   B. Sex–the facet of love
      1. The faces of love
         a. *Agapē*–spiritual love
         b. *Phileo*–social love
         c. *Eros*–sexual love
      2. The fullness of love
         a. Total union of two people (Gen. 2:24)
         b. Sexual, spiritual, social (Gen. 4:1)
   C. Sex–the force of libido
      1. Immensity of sexual drive
      2. Necessity of sexual control

II. Alternative theories of sex
   A. The Puritan ethic
      1. "Sex is slightly shameful"
      2. Produces unhealthy attitudes
      3. Antibiblical (see Prov. 5:15–19)
   B. The *Playboy* ethic
      1. "Sex is fun"
      2. Produces immature activities
      3. Antisocial–hedonism is selfish
   C. The permissive ethic
      1. "Sex is natural"
      2. Produces perverted alliances
      3. Anti-Christian–destroys family structure

III. Christian treatment of sex
   A. The experience of sexual delight
      1. The confines of matrimony (1 Cor. 7:2)
      2. The concept of mutuality (1 Cor. 7:3–5)
   B. The exercise of sexual discipline
      1. Discernment (Matt. 5:29)
         a. Lust in a look
         b. Love isn't lust
      2. Denial (v. 30)
         a. Reject the immoral urge
         b. Renounce the illegal opportunity
      3. Dynamic (see Rom. 8:13; Gal. 5:23)

10

Divorce and the Christian

Matthew 5:31-32

One of modern society's greatest disaster areas is marital and family breakdown. Concepts of divorce are largely responsible. Christ has much to say on the subject.

I. A serious situation
   A. The situation in Christ's day
      1. A liberalized approach (v. 31)
         a. Blatant ignoring of Genesis 2:23–25
         b. Biased interpreting of Deuteronomy 24:1–4
      2. A legalized adultery (Matt. 5:32)
         a. Divorce without biblical basis
         b. Remarriage without divine blessing
   B. The situation in our day
      1. The escalation of the problem—statistics available
      2. The erosion of principles—grounds available
      3. The easing of procedures—methods available

II. A searching statement
- A. Marriage is the divine principle (Mark 10:2–12)
  1. Permanent in the eyes of God (vv. 8–9)
  2. Pleasing to the heart of God (Gen. 1:26–31)
- B. Divorce is a limited privilege
  1. Concession to the hardness of man's heart
  2. Controlled by the strictness of God's law
     a. Fornication that denies the bond
     b. Desertion that destroys the bond (1 Cor. 7:10–16)

III. A spiritual solution
- A. Expose the disaster of secular thinking
  1. Personal
  2. Familial
  3. Social
- B. Expound the design of scriptural teaching
- C. Explode the delusion of selfish thrills
- D. Explore the delights of spiritual triumph (see Ezek. 32:26; Gal. 5:19–24)

11

Communication and the Christian

Matthew 5:33-37

Communications in many sophisticated forms are much in evidence in the modern world. They play a most important role. Christians should have great convictions on the subject.

I. The power of communication
    A. Power to mobilize masses
        1. Biblical examples
            a. Nehemiah 8:1-12
            b. Joshua 3:1-7
        2. Historical examples
            a. Lincoln
            b. Hitler
            c. Churchill
            d. Martin Luther King
    B. Power to initiate ideologies
        1. Biblical examples
            a. Exodus 34:27-36:7
            b. Matthew 6

    2. Historical examples
      a. Lenin
      b. Luther
  C. Power to affect attitudes
    1. Madison Avenue
    2. Political manipulation
  D. Power to create crises
    1. Love
    2. Hate
    3. Fear
    4. Dedication

II. The perversion of communication
  A. Perversion through perjury (Matt. 5:33)
    1. Secular perjury–"forswear"
    2. Spiritual perjury (Eccles. 5:4–5)
  B. Perversion through profanity
    1. Abuse of God's name (Exod. 20:7)
    2. Abuse of God's creation (Matt. 5:34–36)
    3. Evidence of man's unspirituality
  C. Perversion through hypocrisy
    1. Lying to God (Acts 5:3)
    2. Deceiving to man

III. The purity of communication
  A. Purity of motive
    1. Fear of God
    2. Love of mankind
  B. Purity of material
    1. Revealed in Scripture
    2. Reflected in lifestyle
  C. Purity of method
    1. Examination of actions
    2. Evaluation of commitment–Yea is yea, Nay is nay
    3. Eradication of inconsistency

12

Relationships and the Christian

Matthew 5:38-42

Everybody is a member of society. Therefore, relationships are of prime importance to human well-being. Christ spoke much about relationships. These teachings are not to be regarded as principles of international behavior or business ethics but personal principles for members of his kingdom.

   I. Relationship potential
      A. Potential development
         1. Expansion of personality
         2. Expression of personhood
      B. Potential destruction
         1. Destruction of objectives
         2. Denial of opportunities
         3. Disintegration of operation

  II. Relationship pollution
      A. Insistence on preservation of rights

1. Don't insult my dignity (v. 39)
2. Don't interfere with my security (v. 40)
3. Don't invade my privacy (v. 41)
4. Don't infringe on my property (v. 42)

B. Indulgence in practice of reaction
1. Legality of reaction (Exod. 21)
2. Limitation of retaliation (Matt. 5:38)
3. Lust of resistance
   a. Self-vindication
   b. Self-protection
   c. Self-indulgence
   d. Self-aggrandizement

III. Relationship principles
A. Principle of recognition
1. Recognize need
2. Recognize cause
3. Recognize opportunity
B. Principle of responsibility
1. Sees responsibilities as primary
2. Sees rights as secondary
C. Principle of response
1. Self-control (v. 39)
2. Self-denial (v. 40)
3. Self-sacrifice (v. 41)
4. Self-sharing (v. 42)
D. Principle of resurrection
1. As you die to self
2. Live in resurrection

13

Love and the Christian

Matthew 5:43-48

They say that love makes the world go round. The wrong kind of love may, therefore, make it go round the wrong way. Maybe that's part of our modern dilemma. Christ had much to say about Christian love.

I. The magnificence of God's love
    A. According to his nature
        1. His nature is to start things
        2. He shares what he starts (v. 45)
           Note: "*his* sun"
        3. He sends what he shares (v. 45)
           Note: John 3:16
    B. According to man's need
        1. God has the resources
        2. Man has the needs
        3. God loves according to need not character

II. The mediocrity of man's love
   A. Man reserves the right to hate
      1. Curse—wish evil against
      2. Hate—malicious feeling
      3. Despitefully use—accuse falsely (1 Peter 3:16)
      4. Persecute—pursue, put to flight
   B. Man reserves the right to restrict
      1. To certain attitudes (Matt. 5:46)
      2. To special associations (v. 47)
      3. To limited activities (vv. 46–47)

III. The maturity of Christian love
   A. The demands of Christian love
      1. Love God (Luke 10:27)
      2. Love neighbor (Matt. 5:43)
      3. Love enemies (Matt. 5:44)
   B. The display of Christian love
      1. Obedience toward God (John 14:15)
      2. Sacrifice toward neighbors (Luke 10:36–37)
      3. Response toward enemies:
         a. Bless
         b. Do good
         c. Pray
   C. The dynamic of Christian love
      1. Dynamic of divine example (Matt. 5:48)
      2. Dynamic of divine expectation (v. 47)
      3. Dynamic of divine experience (v. 45)
      4. Dynamic of divine enabling (Gal. 5:22)

14

Charity and the Christian

Matthew 6:1-4

Charity, prayer, and fasting were traditionally the means of expressing personal righteousness in Christ's time. They were valid expressions except when abused—it's the same today.

I. Charity—the product of righteousness
   Note: Alms—righteousness (v. 1); charity (vv. 2–4)
   A. Righteousness should be discovered
      1. Recognition of God's righteousness
      2. Rejection of self-righteousness
      3. Repentance of unrighteousness
      4. Reception of Christ's righteousness
   B. Righteousness should be displayed
      1. Conversion (Gal. 1:23–24)
      2. Confession (Matt. 10:32–33)
      3. Communion (1 Cor. 11:26)
      4. Charity (Matt. 5:16; 6:2)

C. Righteousness should be disciplined
   1. Discipline of being aware (Matt. 6:1)
   2. Discipline of being active (v. 2)
   3. Discipline of being alone (v. 3)

II. Charity–the peril of religion
   A. The peril of error (see Luke 18:9–11)
   B. The peril of exhibitionism
      1. Theatrical charity–"to be seen" (Matt. 6:1)
      2. Trumpet charity (v. 2)
   C. The peril of elimination
      1. They have their reward (v. 2)

III. Charity–the promise of reward
   A. Initial reward (Acts 20:35)
   B. Eternal reward (Matt. 6:4; 5:12; 1 Cor. 3:8–14)

15

Prayer and the Christian 1

Matthew 6:5-8

The Lord showed that prayer was expected to be a part of his disciples' lives. Three times he said, "When you pray" not "If you pray." Prayer needs to be understood and practiced, for it is vital.

I. Some aspects of prayer
   A. It was exemplified by the Lord
   B. It was experienced by the church
   C. It is expected of the believer

II. Some activities of prayer
   A. The activity of praise
      1. Man's highest duty
      2. God's deepest joy
   B. The activity of penitence
      1. Evidence of a sensitive spirit
      2. Evidence of a serious soul

    C. The activity of petition
      1. Man's confidence in God
      2. Man's concern for man

III. Some attitudes of prayer
    A. Importunity (Luke 11:5-8)
    B. Tenacity (Luke 18:1-8)
    C. Humility (Luke 18:10-14)
    D. Charity (Matt. 18:21-35)
    E. Simplicity (Matt. 6:5)
    F. Intensity (Matt. 26:41)
    G. Unity (Matt. 18:19)

IV. Some attractions of prayer
    A. Fellowship with the Father
      1. A secret Father (Matt. 6:6)
      2. A seeing Father (v. 6)
      3. A sufficient Father (v. 8)
    B. Effectiveness of the exercise
      1. Refreshment of soul
      2. Relating of problems
      3. Reception of answers

 V. Some abuses of prayer
    A. The "hypocrite" abuse (v. 5)
    B. The "heathen" abuse (v. 7)

16

Prayer and the Christian 2

Matthew 6:9-10

Christ's model prayer includes everything—praise, penitence, and petition. Its six petitions include three concerning the glory of God and three relating to the needs of man: physically, socially and spiritually.

I. Pitfalls to avoid
   A. Performing instead of praying (v. 5)
   B. Phraseology instead of prayer (v. 6)
   C. Prayerlessness—the biggest contemporary pitfall

II. Principles to apply
   A. The basis of prayer
      1. Fatherhood of God is basis (v. 8)
      2. Fatherhood of God is limited (John 8:38–44)

       3. Fatherhood of God through new birth
         (John 1:12–13)
       4. Fatherhood of God by adoption (Gal.
         4:4–7)
   B. The burden of prayer
       1. The glory of God
         Note: *thy* not my
       2. The well-being of all
         Note: *us* not I

III. Person to address
   A. The knowledge of the Father (Matt. 6:32)
   B. The kingdom of the Father (v. 13 KJV)
       1. Glorious kingdom
       2. Powerful kingdom
       3. Eternal kingdom
   C. The kindness of the Father (Matt. 7:7–11)

IV. Petitions to articulate
   A. May your name be honored
       1. By proclamation of its significance
       2. By response to its significance
   B. May your kingdom be completed
       1. Introduced by Christ's ministry (Mark
         1:14–15)
       2. Perpetuated by Christ's disciples (Matt.
         24:14)
       3. Completed by Christ's return (1 Cor.
         15:24–28)
   C. May your will be done (see Matt. 7:21)
       1. How is it done in heaven? (Ps. 103:19–22)
       2. Am I doing it on earth? (Rom. 12:1–2)

17

Prayer and the Christian 3

Matthew 6:11-15

Christ expects his followers to pray, for "prayer is the Christian's vital breath" (James Montgomery). That we should pray is obvious. How and what we should pray has to be learned. Continue to learn in the Lord's model prayer.

I. To pray is to admit
  A. That you have physical needs (v. 11)
    1. They are legitimate needs—"bread"
    2. They are large needs—"daily"
  B. That you have social needs (v. 12)
    1. Because you live in a sinful society
    2. Because you live in a selfish society
  C. That you have spiritual needs (v. 13)
    1. Through the pressure of temptation
    2. Through the presence of evil

II. To pray is to commit
   A. To the God who gives (v. 11)
      1. On the basis of *need* not greed—"bread"
      2. On the basis of *sufficiency* not superfluity—
         "this day"
      3. On the basis of *helping* not hoarding—"us"
   B. To the Father who forgives (v. 12)
      1. To establish a relationship (see Eph. 1:5–7)
      2. To preserve a fellowship (see Luke
         15:19–20)
   C. To the Lord who leads (v. 13)
      1. Who never tempts to sin (James 1:13–15)
      2. Who ever tests to strengthen (1 Peter
         1:6–7)
   D. To the deity who delivers (Matt. 6:13)
      1. From the evil one's domain (Heb. 2:14–15)
      2. From evil's dominion (1 Cor. 10:13)

III. To pray is to submit
   A. To God's power to answer prayer
   B. To God's principles of answered prayer
      1. Being willing to work for bread (2 Thess.
         3:8–10)
      2. Being willing to wipe out debts
         (Matt. 6:14–15)
      3. Being willing to watch your step (Matt.
         26:41)
   C. To God's purposes in answering prayer

18

Fasting and the Christian

Matthew 6:16-18

Fasting has been used as a religious exercise and a political tool for centuries. In our Lord's time it had fallen into ill repute. His statements on the subject are relevant and pungent.

I. The practice of fasting
    A. On a national scale
        1. The Day of Atonement (Lev. 16)
        2. After the exile (Zech. 8:19)
        3. Extraordinary fasts (Joel 2:12-17)
    B. On an individual basis
        1. Moses on the mountain (Exod. 34:27-29)
        2. David in mourning (2 Sam. 1:11-13)
        3. Daniel in confession (Dan. 9:3)
        4. Christ in temptation (Luke 4:2)
        5. Paul in extremities (2 Cor. 6:5)
    C. On an ecclesiastical basis
        1. Before major decisions (Acts 14:23)
        2. Before major developments (Acts 13:2-3)

II. The problems of fasting
   A. It may be ritual without reality (Isa. 58:1–7)
   B. It may be performance demanding recognition
      (Matt. 6:16)
   C. It may be activity anticipating God's favor
      (Luke 18:11–12)

III. The place of fasting
   A. Its validity in today's world
      1. Christ's principles are timeless
      2. Today's problems are serious
   B. Its value in today's world
      1. The physical value
         a. The body must be cared for (1 Cor.
            6:13–15)
         b. The body must be controlled (1 Cor.
            9:27)
      2. The spiritual value
         a. Self-denial a Christian principle (Matt.
            16:24)
         b. Self-control a Christian virtue (Gal.
            5:23)
         c. Self-humiliation a Christian imperative
            (James 4:7–10)
      3. The national value
         a. A corrupt nation needs a concerned
            church
         b. A concerned church affects a corrupt
            nation
      4. The social value
         a. Indulgence in the presence of need is
            gross sin (Luke 16:19)
         b. Denying and sharing are evidences of
            God's grace (Acts)

19

Wealth and the Christian

Matthew 6:19-24

The acquisition and administration of wealth demands a great deal of attention. We have a special responsibility, for the United States, with 7 percent of the world's population, has 50 percent of the world's wealth. It needs careful handling.

I. The acquisition of wealth
   A. Man has rights that incorporate wealth
      Note: inferred, not stated in Scripture
      (see Exod. 20:13-17)
   B. Man has needs that require wealth, for example, food, shelter, security
   C. Man has abilities that produce wealth

II. The abuses of wealth
   A. The means of purchasing
      1. Possessions
      2. People

  3. Prestige
  4. Popularity
 B. The means of projecting
  1. "Success"
  2. Self-sufficiency

III. The administration of wealth
  A. The capitalist's view
  B. The socialist's view
  C. The Christian's view:
   1. Alert to the dangers
    a. Money can lead you to materialism
       (Matt. 6:21)
    b. Money can mislead you into myopia
       (vv. 22–23; see Mark 10:17–22; Luke
       12:19–20; Luke 16:19–22)
    c. Money can manipulate you into
       mammonism (Matt. 6:24)
   2. Aware of the differences
    a. Between earth and heaven (vv. 19–20)
    b. Between light and darkness (vv. 22–23)
    c. Between God and mammon (v. 24)
   3. Appreciative of the disciplines
    a. Of seeing it scripturally (1 Tim. 6:17)
    b. Of sharing it joyfully (2 Cor. 9:7)
    c. Of saving it wisely (2 Cor. 12:14)
    d. Of spending it carefully (Luke 16:1)

20

Anxiety and the Christian

Matthew 6:25-34

Anxiety and joy don't mix. Neither do anxiety and liberty. But Christ promised both joy and liberty; therefore, something has to be done about anxiety.

I. Common areas of anxiety
   Note: "take no thought" (vv. 25, 31, 34) literally, "be not anxious"
   A. Concern is commended
      1. In marriage (1 Cor. 7:32, 34)
      2. In membership (1 Cor. 12:25)
      3. In ministry (2 Cor. 11:28)
      4. In missions (Phil. 2:20)
   B. Anxiety is condemned
      Note: "life"–Greek, *psychē* (Matt. 6:25)
      1. In personal finance (vv. 19–21)
      2. In personal food (v. 25)
      3. In personal fashions (v. 25)

    4. In personal fitness (v. 25)
    5. In personal future (v. 27)

II. Christ's attitude to anxiety
  A. An exercise in futility (v. 27)
    Anxiety won't change anything.
    Note: "stature"–literally, "life span"
  B. An evidence of faithlessness (v. 30)
    1. Despite God's obvious purposes (v. 25)
      a. He made life and body
      b. Therefore, he can make bread and
         butter
    2. Despite God's obvious providence (v. 26)
      a. In realm of nature
      b. In relationship to man
         Note: man more responsible than birds
         and lilies

III. Christian's answer to anxiety
  A. Accept divine providence
    Note: "therefore" (vv. 25, 31, 34)
  B. Adopt divine priorities (v. 33) "first the
    kingdom"
  C. Anticipate divine promises (v. 33)
  D. Apply divine principles (v. 34)
    1. Live one day at a time

21

Priorities and the Christian

Matthew 6:33

To say "first things first" is not difficult. But to decide what is first and then to make it first is another matter. "Major on majors and minor on minors" is great but what is major and what is minor? The answer to these questions and the application of the answers is of utmost importance.

I. Recognize your priorities
   A. By your activities–for example, "laying up in store" (v. 19)
   B. By your anxieties
      1. Finance (vv. 19–21)
      2. Food (v. 25)
      3. Fashion (v. 25)
      4. Fitness (v. 25)
      5. Future (v. 27)
   C. By your ambitions–for example, "seek"; also "desire" (Phil. 4:17); "endeavor" (Acts 16:10)

II. Rate your priorities
   A. Activities in the light of eternity–"treasure in heaven" (v. 20)
   B. Anxieties in the light of Providence–"your heavenly Father knows" (v. 32)
   C. Ambitions in the light of kingdom–"first the kingdom" (v. 33)
      1. The kingdom must be experienced (see John 3:3–5)
      2. The kingdom must be expressed (see 1 Cor. 4:20; Rom. 14:17)
      3. The kingdom must be extended (see Matt. 6:10; Matt. 24:14)

III. Relate your priorities
   A. By correct application
      1. By applying the eternal to the earthly–for example, in the area of finance
      2. By applying providence to problems–for example, in the area of family
      3. By applying the spiritual to the secular–for example, in the area of future
   B. By constant anticipation (Matt. 6:33)
      1. If we major on the all-important
      2. He will look after the less important

22

Criticism and the Christian

Matthew 7:1-6

God has given us critical abilities. They are to be used correctly and carefully. Some usages of critical ability are flatly condemned. Others are forcefully commanded. Christians need great discernment in the exercise of these abilities.

I. The criticism that Christ condemned
   A. Its characteristics
      1. Its objective is to destroy
         a. Reputation
         b. Ministry
         c. Effectiveness
      2. It operates on a double standard
         Note: the worst kind of "critical" is "hypocritical"
   B. Its condemnation
      1. Condemned because contradictory to
         a. Edification

    b. Fellowship
    c. Love
   2. Condemned because counterproductive
    a. Strife (Matt. 7:2)
    b. Schism (Gal. 5:15; James 3:13–16)
  C. Its causes
   1. Jealousy
   2. Pride
   3. Guilt

II. The criticism that Christ commended
  A. Self-criticism
   1. Consciousness of personal condition (Matt. 7:4)
   2. Concern to improve condition (v. 5)
   3. Comparison of own and other's condition (v. 3)
   4. Constructive ministry in view (v. 5)
  B. Spiritual discernment (v. 6)
   1. Discern spiritual condition of others
    Note: "dogs, swine!"
   2. Discern spiritual abilities of others
    Note: "trample, turn"
   3. Discern spiritual truth applicable to others
    Note: "holy, pearls"

III. The criticism that Christ commanded
  A. In the exercise of God-given authority
   1. The law
   2. The family
  B. In the exercise of God-given ministry
   1. The church
   2. The society
  C. In the expression of God-given personality
   Note: be critical of your own criticism

23

Confidence and the Christian

Matthew 7:7-12

Self-confidence is ultimately disastrous. Lack of confidence is not much better. Only confidence that derives from God will produce the correct blend of humility and confidence that life demands.

I. The context of living
   Note: getting things out of context produces error, imbalance, absurdity, and chaos
   A. The spiritual context of life—"Father in Heaven" (v. 11)
   B. The moral context of life—"Law and the Prophets" (v. 12)
   C. The relational context of life—"that men should do" (v. 12)
   D. The personal context of life—"your children" (v. 11)

II. The challenge of living
   A. The immensity of the challenge
      Where do we find . . .
     1. Desire for the spiritual?
     2. Discipline for the moral?
     3. Dynamic for the relational?
     4. Discernment for the personal?
   B. The inadequacy of the challenged
      Note: "ye being evil" (v. 11)
     1. We have inherited an evil heart (Mark 7:23)
     2. We have inhabited an evil world (Gal. 1:4)
     3. We are inhibited by an evil one (Matt. 13:19)

III. The confidence of living
   A. Derived in the fact of God (Matt. 7:11)
     1. His greatness
     2. His graciousness
     3. His giving-ness
   B. Developed in the faith of man (v. 7)
     1. A faith that prays–"ask"
     2. A faith that pursues–"seek"
     3. A faith that persists–"knock"
       Note: literally, go on asking, seeking, knocking
   C. Demonstrated in the fruit of behavior fulfilling the law and the prophets

24

Discipline and the Christian

Matthew 7:13-14

Discipline, self-control, and sober-mindedness are not everybody's favorite topics. But they are an important part of Christian behavior. Christ made it clear that commitment to him is through a "straight gate" and along a "narrow way."

I. The discipline of discernment
   A. The two ends
      1. Life (John 10:10; Rom. 6:23)
      2. Destruction (1 Cor. 1:18; 2 Cor. 4:3; Matt. 26:8)
   B. The two experiences
      1. The narrow way (Matt. 4:19; John 9:4)
      2. The broad way (Judg. 21:25; 2 Tim. 3:1–5)

C. The two entrances
  1. The straight gate (John 14:6)
  2. The wide gate (latitudinarianism, universalism)
D. The two environs
  1. The minority experience–"few there be"
  2. The majority experience–"many there be"

II. The discipline of decision
  Note: relates to "gate" and "way"
  A. A matter of cognizance–"mind"
  B. A matter of courage–"emotion" (see Luke 13:24)
  C. A matter of choice–"will"

III. The discipline of discipleship
  Note: "narrow"–Greek, *thlibō* (see Mark 3:9; 2 Cor. 4:8; 1 Thess. 3:4; Matt. 16:24)
  A. The narrow way of commitment–"after me"
  B. The narrow way of crucifixion–"deny himself"
  C. The narrow way of confession–"take up the cross"
  D. The narrow way of continuance–"follow me" (remember Matthew 11:28–30)

25

Vigilance and the Christian

Matthew 7:15-20

The condition on which God has given liberty to man is eternal vigilance . . ." (John Philpot Curran). In the area of spiritual experience vigilance is of great importance. "Beware!"

I. Be clear about your vulnerability
  A. Because Satan is a tyrant
    1. Satan as lion (1 Peter 5:8)
    2. Satan as light (2 Cor. 11:13–14)
    3. Satan as liar (John 8:44)
  B. Because the world is treacherous
    1. Its attractions are obvious (Eph. 2:2)
    2. Its attacks are insidious (Eph. 6:12–13)
  C. Because the flesh is a traitor
    1. An antagonist of the spirit (Gal. 5:17–23)
    2. An ally of Satan (Rom. 7:24)

II. Be careful about your vigilance
   A. Prophets are to be checked
   Because false prophets are:
    1. Dangerous (Matt. 7:15)
    2. Deceptive–"sheep"
    3. Divisive (Acts 20:28–31; Rev. 2:2)
    4. Destructive–"wolves"
   B. Pronouncements are to be challenged (1 John 4:1–3) on the basis of
    1. Deity of Christ
    2. Incarnation of Christ
    3. Confession of Christ
    4. Spirit of Christ
     (see 1 Cor. 12:3)
     Note: Gnostic heresy of first century and similarities in twentieth century
   C. Production is to be critically evaluated (vv. 16–20)
    1. The fruits of profession
    2. The fruits of production
     a. Evidence of the spirit (Gal. 5:22–23)
     b. Activity of the spirit (Eph. 4:1–16)

III. Be concerned about your victory
   A. Don't heed seducing spirits (1 Tim. 4:1)
   B. Do heed sure word of Scripture (1 Tim. 4:13; 2 Peter 1:19)
   Note: Keep the balance:
    1. So careless in Laish they lost their lives (Judg. 18:7)
    2. So careful in Ephesus they lost their love (Rev. 2:1–2)

26

Obedience and the Christian

Matthew 7:21-23

Obedience is not the most popular of topics, but it is one of the most necessary. For Christians know that obedience is the evidence of faith, the criterion of judgment, and the acknowledgement of lordship.

I. The significance of obedience
   A. In our Savior's example
      1. The motivation for service (John 6:38)
      2. The motivation for suffering (Matt. 26:39; Heb. 5:7–9)
      3. The motivation for sacrifice (Phil. 2:8)
   B. In our spiritual experience
      1. An evidence of repentance–valid repentance produces visible results (Acts 26:20)
      2. An end product of regeneration
         a. By nature children of disobedience (Eph. 2:2)
         b. By new nature children of obedience (1 Peter 1:13–14)

3. An expression of relationships
   a. Relationship to the Lord (Luke 6:46;
      1 Cor. 12:3; Rom. 10:9)
   b. Relationship of love (John 14:15)
   c. Relationship of faith (Eph. 2:8–10;
      James 2:14–26)
   d. Relationship of knowledge (John 13:17)
      Note: Relationship is "to know and to
      be known" (Matt. 7:23)
C. In our solemn expectation—"in that day"
   1. God has appointed a day (Acts 17:31)
   2. The judge has appointed a criterion
      (Matt. 7:21)

II. The substitute for obedience
   A. Superficial worship—"Lord, Lord"
   B. Spurious witness—"in thy name"
   C. Spectacular work
      1. Prophecy
      2. Exorcism
      3. Miracles
         Note: Characterized as "lawlessness" (v. 23)

III. The steps to obedience
   A. To desire God's will
   B. To discover God's will
   C. To do God's will

27

Wisdom and the Christian

Matthew 7:24-29

Everything seems to be crumbling like houses built on sand. Some sensible, secure, stable people are needed to stand in the chaos. Christ said it is the wise who stand.

I. Wisdom makes people sensible (v. 24)
   A. They pay attention to Christ's teaching
      1. It projects authority (v. 29)
      2. It produces astonishment (v. 28)
         Note: *ekplēssō* (Gk.)–literally, "strike out"
   B. They mix action with Christ's teaching
      Note: *sophos* (Gk.)–"theoretical insight";
      phronimōs–"practical prudence"
      1. In terms of preservation (10:16)
      2. In terms of proclamation (24:45)
      3. In terms of preparation (25:2)

    C. They resist antagonism to Christ's teaching
       Note: *mōros* (Gk.)–"foolish"
      1. Antagonism through disinterest
      2. Antagonism through disbelief
      3. Antagonism through disobedience
        (see James 1:21–25)

II. Wisdom makes people secure (Matt. 7:24)
    A. A secure base
      1. The rock of Christ's truth (10:17–20)
      2. The rock of Christ's teaching (7:24)
        (see Eph. 3:17; Col. 1:23; 1 Peter 5:10)
    B. A secure building
      1. The building of Christian character (1 Cor. 10:23)
      2. The building of Christian community (Acts 9:31)
      3. The building of Christian concern (1 Thess. 5:11)

III. Wisdom makes people stable (Matt. 7:25)
    A. The areas of testing
      1. Doctrinal (7:15)
      2. Personal (5:28)
      3. Relational (5:24)
      4. Practical (6:19)
      5. Spiritual (6:24)
    B. The ability to triumph
      (see 2 Cor. 2:12–14)

Part **2**

Discipleship

28

The Meaning of Discipleship

John 1:35-51

Jesus began his public ministry by calling disciples to himself. He concluded it by commissioning his disciples to go into the world and "disciple all nations."

I. The meaning of discipleship
   Note: the relationship between *didaskalos* and *mathētēs*
   A. Disciples of Greeks–a discipleship of philosophy
   B. Disciples of Moses–a discipleship of principle
   C. Disciples of Pharisees–a discipleship of procedures
   D. Disciples of John the Baptist–a discipleship of protest
   E. Disciples of Christ–a discipleship of person
      1. Chosen to be with him (Mark 3:14)
      2. Invited to come to him (Matt. 11:28–30)
      3. Called to follow him (John 1:43)

II. The making of disciples (John 6)
    A. Christ's ministry to the curious (v. 2)
        1. A ministry of works to establish credibility
        2. A ministry of miracles to attract attention
        3. A ministry of compassion to meet need
        4. A ministry of teaching to promote belief
    B. Christ's ministry to the convinced (v. 29)
        1. To reveal his true identity (v. 33)
        2. To relate his true purpose (v. 38)
        3. To require their true response (v. 47)
    C. Christ's ministry to the committed (v. 66)
        1. Committed to the uniqueness of his person (v. 69)
        2. Committed to the uniqueness of his passion (v. 53)
        3. Committed to the uniqueness of his promise (v. 58)

III. The measure of discipleship
    A. The reality of relationship
        1. Obedience to him
        2. Dependence upon him
    B. The depth of dedication
        1. An exclusive dedication
        2. An exhaustive dedication

29

The Making of a Disciple

Luke 5:1-11

The Lord called people to himself in different ways, but in each case there were fundamental realities. These need to be understood because they still apply.

I. The revelation reality
   A. The importance of the word of God (v. 1)
      1. A touch of reality
      2. A voice of authority (4:31–36)
      3. A word of security (4:18–21)
   B. The impact of the word of God
      1. It challenges us to obedience (5:4–5)
      2. It charms us to amazement (4:22)

II. The reaction reality
   A. To the Lord
      1. What was said
         a. Master—Greek, *epistatēs* (5:5)
         b. Lord—Greek, *kurios* (v. 8)

    2. What was done (v. 8)
      a. An act of contrition
      b. An act of confession
      c. An act of consternation (v. 10)
  B. To himself (v. 8)
    1. The gaining of correct perspective
    2. The discovery of proper evaluation

III. The regeneration reality (v. 10)
  A. A sense of composure
    1. Enjoying the Lord's favor (4:19)
    2. Escaping the world's fear (4:10)
  B. A sense of commission
    1. Men rather than fish
    2. Catching for God not devil (cf. 2 Tim. 2:26)
  C. A sense of commitment
    1. Leaving the secondary for the primary
    2. Following the Master not the inclination

30

The Maturing of a Disciple

Luke 9:1-6, 18-27

When Peter and his friends agreed to become Christ's disciples, they knew they were committing themselves to following Christ, but they didn't know where he would take them. They soon found out!

I. A clearer perception of Christ's ministry (vv. 18–27)
   A. Popular perceptions (v. 19)
      1. John the Baptist resurrected
      2. Other prophets returned
      3. Messianic activity suspected (Mal. 4:5)
   B. Personal perceptions (Luke 9:20–22)
      1. The challenge to come to a conclusion
      2. The challenge to make a confession
      3. The challenge to confront a cross
      4. The challenge to count the cost (v. 23)
      5. The challenge to contemplate the cloud (vv. 28–36)

II. A fuller appreciation of Christian mission (vv. 1–6)
   A. No confusion about their priorities
      1. Announcing the kingdom of God (v. 2)
      2. Attacking the kingdom of Satan (v. 1)
      3. Addressing the need of mankind (v. 6)
   B. No illusion about their problems
      1. The strength of the opposition (v. 1; 10:3)
      2. The seriousness of the situation (vv. 3–4)
      3. The size of the commission (10:1–2)
      4. The shortage of the cooperation (10:2)
   C. No evasion of their privileges
      1. He gave them authority (v. 1)
      2. He granted them power

III. A deeper evaluation of Christian motivation (vv. 23–27)
   A. The place of selflessness (v. 23)
   B. The probability of suffering (v. 23)
   C. The principal of sacrifice (vv. 24–25)
   D. The proclamation of stand (v. 26)
   E. The prospect of splendor (v. 27)

31

The Mistakes of a Disciple

Luke 9:33-62

That human beings are error prone is an unfortunate fact of life. But treated properly, mistakes can be turned to good use, and "learning by mistakes" has proven to be a very effective educational tool, although expensive and sometimes painful. The disciples of Jesus certainly made their share of mistakes, but the Master taught them much through the experience.

I. The catalog of mistakes
   A. Desiring an inappropriate experience (v. 33)
   B. Attempting an impossible task (v. 37)
   C. Creating an inexcusable tension (v. 46)
   D. Making an inaccurate judgment (v. 49)
   E. Proposing an intolerable action (v. 51)
   F. Displaying an inadequate commitment (v. 57)
   G. Projecting an immature attitude (Luke 10:17)

II. The causes of mistakes
   A. Misguided enthusiasm
      1. The enthusiasm of enjoyment (9:33)
      2. The enthusiasm of involvement (v. 49)
      3. The enthusiasm of commitment (v. 54)
   B. Misdirected confidence
      1. The confidence of experience (Note: Mark 9:29)
      2. The confidence of success (Luke 10:20)
   C. Misplaced ambition
      1. The ambition to be great (9:46)
      2. The determination to be greatest
   D. Misjudged priorities
      1. Priorities of comfort (v. 58)
      2. Priorities of convenience (v. 60)
      3. Priorities of commitment (v. 62)

III. The consequences of mistakes
   A. Reactions to mistakes
      1. Suggestion ignored–idealistic Peter
      2. Frustration expressed–powerless disciples
      3. Misapprehensions corrected–ambitious disciples
      4. Actions forbidden–forbidding disciples
      5. Attitudes rebuked–condemning disciples
      6. Mistakes challenged–inadequate disciples
      7. Caution demanded–exhilarated disciples
   B. Results of mistakes
      1. A lesson on balance
      2. A lesson on power
      3. A lesson on humility
      4. A lesson on acceptance
      5. A lesson on tolerance
      6. A lesson on depth
      7. A lesson on perspective

32

The Mind of a Disciple

Luke 11:1-13

The mind of man is hidden from view, but his actions are full of clues. When a man asks to be taught to pray, this speaks loud and clear about his state of mind. Disciples of Christ are such people.

I. Prayer as a declaration of discipleship
   A. The impact of Christ's example
      1. His regular habit of prayer (5:16)
      2. His specific experiences of prayer
         a. His baptism (3:21)
         b. His decisions (6:12)
         c. His transfiguration (9:28)
         d. His passion (22:41)
   B. The importance of Christ's expectations
      1. His teaching on principles (18:1)
      2. His teaching on practicalities (18:9)

II. Prayer as a declaration of desire
   A. A desire for personal growth (11:1)

       1. The learning of new things
       2. The expanding of new experiences
   B. A desire for relational depth (v. 2)
       1. Knowing the Father
       2. Growing in that knowing
   C. A desire for spiritual truth (v. 2)
       1. The truth in the "name"
       2. The truth in the "name" being known
       3. The truth in the "name" being honored
   D. A desire for eternal breadth (v. 2)
       1. The breadth of the kingdom's embrace
       2. The length of the kingdom's extent
       3. The height of the kingdom's glory
       4. The depth of the kingdom's significance

III. Prayer as a declaration of dependence
   A. Recognizing the reality of dependence
   B. Articulating the admission of dependence
   C. Stipulating the spheres of dependence (vv. 3–4)
       1. The sphere of physical need
       2. The sphere of personal forgiveness
       3. The sphere of interpersonal relations
       4. The sphere of spiritual conflict
   D. Indicating the importance of dependence (vv. 5–8)
       1. Indicating a sense of urgency
       2. Demonstrating a sense of importunity
   E. Discovering the delights of dependence (vv. 9–13)
       1. Asking and being answered
       2. Seeking and being shown
       3. Knocking and being accepted
       4. Requesting and being overwhelmed

33

The Major of a Disciple

Luke 12:22-40

The interests and objectives that fill our lives fall into major and minor categories. The disciple's major is clearly stated—it is "seek ye first the kingdom."

I. Monitoring majors and minors
   A. Recognizing that majors and minors exist
   B. Identifying these majors and minors
      1. Anxieties identify majors and minors
         a. Anxiety about the future (vv. 4–7)
         b. Anxiety about friends (v. 8)
         c. Anxiety about family (v. 13)
         d. Anxiety about food (vv. 22–24)
         e. Anxiety about fitness (v. 25)
         f. Anxiety about fashion (vv. 27–28)
         g. Anxiety about finance (v. 34)
      2. Activities identify majors and minors
         a. Activities for profit (vv. 17–18)
         b. Activities for pleasure (v. 19)

    3. Ambitions identify majors and minors
       a. Ambitions to be (v. 19)
       b. Ambitions to do
       c. Ambitions to have

II. Measuring majors and minors
  A. The kingdom is the standard of measurement
    1. It is to be desired (v. 31)
    2. It is to be embraced (v. 32)
  B. The kingdom is the basis of reassessment
    1. Death or hell? (vv. 4–7)
    2. Friends or God? (v. 8)
    3. Life or things? (v. 15)

III. Manifesting majors and minors
  A. New perspectives
    1. The kingdom becomes all-important
    2. The less important less
    3. The more important more
    4. The unimportant un!
  B. New priorities
    1. The priority of giving (v. 33)
    2. The priority of burning (v. 35)
    3. The priority of expecting (v. 36)
    4. The priority of serving (v. 37)

34

The Marks of a Disciple

John 13:34-35; 15:1-8

Christ expected his disciples to make a lasting impression on their world. Their weapons were to be distinctive and attractive lives. He still has the same expectation.

I. The mark of brotherly love (13:34–35)
   A. Christ's love for his disciples
      1. A model
         a. A model of humility (13:1)
         b. A model of patience (21:20)
         c. A model of forgiveness (Gal. 2:20)
         d. A model of understanding (John 11:5)
         e. A model of compassion (Mark 10:21)
      2. A motivation
         a. Christ's love introduced me to the Father
         b. Christ's love invited me into the family

B. Disciples' love for each other
  1. It is demanded
  2. It is demanding
     a. Love must be guarded by truth (Eph. 4:15)
     b. Love must be governed by wisdom (Phil. 1:9)
  3. It is demonstrative (1 John 3:11–24)
     a. The sacrificial aspect (v. 16)
     b. The sharing aspect (v. 17)
     c. The submissive aspect (v. 24)

II. The mark of productive living (John 15:1–9)
  A. The significance of the vine (v. 1)
     1. The vine exists to produce
  B. The status of the branches (v. 4)
     1. The means of the vine's production
  C. The source of the life (v. 5)
     1. Christ himself is the dynamic
  D. The secret of the productivity
     1. Abiding in Christ (v. 7)
     2. Abiding in love of Christ (v. 9)
     3. Abiding in Word of God (v. 7)
     4. Abiding in attitude of prayer (v. 7)

35

The Mandate of a Disciple

Matthew 28:16-20

All four Gospels record slightly different versions of Christ's instructions to his disciples concerning their responsibilities during his absence. The Book of Acts records their response, and church history fills in the details up to modern times.

I. Concluding instructions to the disciples
   A. There's something I want you to know
      1. Concerning authority
         a. It has been given to me
         b. It is relevant in heaven
         c. It is operative on earth
      2. Concerning security
         a. I am with you
         b. To the end of the age
      3. Concerning identity
         a. You will operate "in the name"

B. There's something I want you to do
   1. Make disciples of all nations
      a. By going
      b. By teaching
      c. By baptizing
C. There's somewhere I want you to go (Acts 1:8)
   1. Jerusalem–the place of failure
   2. Judea–the place of difficulty
   3. Samaria–the place of opposition
   4. The uttermost parts–the place of challenge

II. Contrasting reactions by the disciples
  A. Some worshiped
    1. Worship as a matter of style
    2. Worship as a matter of substance
  B. Some doubted
    1. The conflict of being in two minds
    2. The contradiction of having two minds
    3. The confusion in showing two minds

Part 3

How Jesus Explained It

36

Forgiveness

Luke 7:39-50

While dining with a Pharisee, Jesus was visited by a woman of questionable morals. He used the opportunity to tell a story that illustrates the meaning of forgiveness.

I. The failure that needs forgiveness
   A. We are in God's debt
   B. We are responsible for our debt
   C. We have incurred various degrees of debt (v. 41)
   D. We are incapable of repaying our debt (v. 42)
   E. Sin is the nature of our debt (v. 48)
   F. Judgment is the result of our debt
   G. Forgiveness is our only hope

II. The faith that receives forgiveness
   A. Only God can forgive sins (v. 49)
   B. Only the forgiver can assume the debt

C. Only the debtor can acknowledge the debt
D. Only faith can accept the cancellation of debt

III. The freedom that follows forgiveness
   A. Freedom from fear (v. 50)
   B. Freedom from self-consciousness
   C. Freedom to love unreservedly
   D. Freedom to forgive

37

Receptiveness

Luke 8:4-15

It is not uncommon for preachers to be criticized by their hearers, but Jesus pointed out that hearers are always evaluated by the word preached. Soil may evaluate seed, but seed also evaluated soil.

I. The seed is the Word
  A. The general abilities of seed
     1. Seminal abilities—life of the embryo
     2. Survival abilities—enduring elements
     3. Dispersal abilities—innumerable ways of "scattering"
     4. Potential abilities—capacity to be dormant
  B. The special abilities of the Word
     1. Word of the kingdom (Matt. 13:19)
     2. Word of God (Luke 8:11)
     3. Word made flesh (John 1:14)
     4. Word of life (Phil. 2:16)

II. The soil is the world
    A. The properties of the soil
       Note: One meter of rich soil may contain one billion organisms
       1. Relieving
       2. Recycling
       3. Reproducing
       4. Releasing
    B. The preparation of the soil
       1. Wayside soil (Luke 8:5)
       2. Rocky soil (v. 6)
       3. Cluttered soil (v. 7)
       4. Good soil (v. 8)
    C. The productivity of the soil
       1. Nonproductive wayside soil (v. 12)
          a. Unreceptive soil
          b. Unprotected seed
       2. Nonproductive rocky soil (v. 13)
          a. No root
          b. No reality
       3. Nonproductive cluttered soil (v. 14)
          a. No priority
          b. No harvest
       4. Productive good soil (v. 15)
          a. Receive warmly
          b. Grasp thoroughly
          c. Retain consistently

III. The sowing is the witnessing

38

Neighborliness

Luke 10:25-37

One day a Jewish leader, well versed in the Mosaic law, stood up in one of Christ's meetings and asked a question designed to trick him. The result of the interruption was a simple parable full of profound teaching on neighborliness

I. The place of neighborliness in the divine economy
   A. A requirement of the law of God
      1. Law's insistence of love for God and man (v. 27)
      2. Law as a means of inheriting God's blessing (v. 28)
   B. A reflection of the love of God
      1. God's care for individuals
      2. God's concern for society
   C. A recognition of the creativity of God
      1. People are part of the divine intentions
      2. People are projections of the divine image

    D. A result of the acknowledgment of God
       1. Loving God involves loving what God
         loves
    E. A reminder of the judgment of God
       1. By the law is the knowledge of sin

II. The problems of neighborliness in human
    experience
    A. Insignificant comprehension
       1. Importance of neighborliness
       2. Meaning of neighborliness
    B. Inappropriate commitment
       1. Commitment to limited neighborliness–
         lawyer
       2. Commitment to limited involvement–priest
       3. Commitment to limited commitment–
         Levite
    C. Inadequate compassion
       1. Compassion governed by fear
       2. Compassion controlled by finance

III. The practice of neighborliness in Christian ethics
    A. Christian neighborliness in principle
       1. Law says: "Do this and live."
       2. Grace says: "Live and do this."
    B. Christian neighborliness in practice
       1. Its costly nature
       2. Its comprehensive nature
       3. Its continuing nature

39

Prayerfulness

Luke 11:1-13

John the Baptist taught his disciples to pray, and some of Jesus' followers thought he should do the same thing. He obliged them by reminding them of the prayer he had already taught them and by telling a humorous parable that vividly illustrates prayer in action.

I. The context of prayerfulness
   A. The exercise of a free will–you don't *have* to pray!
   B. The expression of an intimate relationship– "Father"
   C. The exaltation of a heavenly Father–"in heaven"
   D. The exposition of a personal priority–"Thy name, etc."
   E. The exhibition of a corporate involvement– "our"
   F. The explanation of a personal concern–"give"

II. The confidence of prayerfulness
    A. The roots of confidence
        1. An accurate view of God
           a. Not a grumpy friend (see vv. 5–7)
           b. Not a ghoulish father (see vv. 11–12)
           Note: "How much more" (v. 13)
        2. A growing appreciation of prayer
           a. The intrinsic worth of prayer
           b. The inspiration of answered prayer
    B. The fruits of confidence
        1. Humbleness–"asking" (v. 9)
        2. Earnestness–"seeking" (v. 9)
        3. Forcefulness–"knocking" (v. 9)
        4. Shamelessness–"importunity" (v. 8)

III. The consequences of prayerfulness
    A. The Father is revered
    B. The pray-er is refreshed
    C. The prayer is recorded
    D. The answer is received (v. 9)
        1. Not necessarily as expected
        2. Not necessarily as requested
        3. But always as needed
           a. "As many as he needeth" (v. 8)
           b. "Good gifts" (v. 13)
           c. "The Holy Spirit" (v. 13)

40

Covetousness

Luke 12:13-21

In the midst of a serious teaching session Jesus was interrupted by a man who wanted him to intervene in a family financial dispute. He not only refused but also took the opportunity to express himself on the subject of covetousness, which he recognized as the real problem.

I. The scriptural identification of covetousness
   Note: *epithumeom* (Gk.)–"passionate desire"
   philarguria (Gk.)—"love of mercy"
   pleonexia (Gk.)—"to have more"
   A. An identification of the causes of covetousness
      1. An evil heart (Mark 7:22)
      2. A reprobate mind (Rom. 1:29)
      3. A callous conscience (Eph. 4:19)
      4. An apostate spirit (Col. 3:5)
   B. An identification of the consequences of covetousness

1. Condemnation by God (Exod. 20:17; Rom. 7:7)
2. Conflict in society (Luke 12:14; 1 Tim. 6:10)
3. Confusion in lifestyle (Luke 12:15)

II. The Savior's illustration of covetousness
  A. The success of a covetous man
    1. Rich
    2. Retired
    3. Respected
  B. The failure of a covetous man
    1. The failure of his egotism—I, my
    2. The failure of his naturalism—God, soul
    3. The failure of his materialism—whose goods?
    4. The failure of his hedonism—eat, drink, and take it easy

III. The specific instructions regarding covetousness
  A. Take heed (v. 15)
    1. Not to disguise it (v. 13; 1 Thess. 2:5)
    2. Not to discount it (see I.B. above)
    3. Not to discuss it (Eph. 5:3)
  B. Take action
    Note: "beware" (be on your guard against)
    1. By evaluating your attitudes
      a. To your own possessions
      b. To others' possessions
    2. By examining your commitment
      a. To yourself
      b. To God (Luke 12:21)
    3. By balancing your checkbook
    4. By making your will
    5. By checking your budget

41

Readiness

Luke 12:35-48

When Christ taught the people of his day, it became very obvious that many of them were so caught up with the secular, the immediate, the temporal, and the personal aspects of their lives that they were unprepared for life in its sacred, ultimate, eternal, and divine dimensions. He warned people to get ready.

I. Some pertinent information about readiness
   A. The Father is all ready (Heb. 11:16)
   B. The Son is getting ready (John 14:2)
   C. The Spirit is revealing readiness (1 Cor. 2:9–10)
   D. The Christians should be ready (Titus 3:1)

II. Some powerful incentives to readiness
   A. The imminence of Christ's return
      1. The certainty of his return (Luke 12:40)
         a. To fulfill his promises
         b. To complete his purposes

2. The uncertainty of his return (v. 40)
   Note: "the signs of the times" (Mark 13)
   a. Signs are not designed to state the date!
   b. Signs are designed to prepare the state of mind!

B. The importance of Christian responsibility
   1. Responsibility in the Lord's absence
   2. Responsibility as the Lord's agents
      a. Slave (Luke 12:37)
      b. Goodman (v. 39)
      c. Steward (v. 42)
      d. Household (v. 42)
      e. Menservants, maidens (v. 45)

C. The implications of certain retribution
   1. Reward for the faithful
      a. Provision (v. 37)
      b. Promotion (v. 44)
   2. Requital for the unfaithful
      a. Related to offense (v. 45)
      b. Related to opportunity (vv. 47–48)

III. Some practical indications for readiness
   A. In terms of attitude
      1. Loins girded
      2. Lights burning (v. 35)
   B. In terms of activity
      1. Ready to work (2 Tim. 2:21)
      2. Ready to witness (1 Peter 3:15)
      3. Ready to wait (Luke 12:36)

42

Fruitfulness

Luke 13:1-9

Jesus' simple story about the fig tree that didn't produce and the reprieve that the owner of the vineyard granted to it is a striking reminder of the truth that God patiently waits for fruitfulness—but not indefinitely.

I. Fruitfulness is an expression of reality
   Note: "hypocrites" (Luke 12:56)
   A. The unreality of Christ's hearers
      1. Unreality about fire (vv. 49–50)
      2. Unreality about friction (vv. 51–53)
      3. Unreality about foresight (vv. 54–56)
      4. Unreality about forgiveness (vv. 57–59)
      5. Unreality about fate (13:1–5)
   B. The reality of Christ's followers
      1. They perceived the truth
      2. They produced the fruit

II. Fruitfulness is an evidence of repentance
  A. The nature of repentance
     1. An initial change of mind (v. 5)
     2. A continual attitude of mind (v. 3)
  B. The necessity for repentance
     1. Except you repent you perish (vv. 3–5)
     2. When you repent you produce (Matt. 3:8)

III. Fruitfulness is an example of relationship
  A. Unfruitfulness is the rejection of this relationship
  B. Fruitfulness is the response to the relationship
     1. Relationship acknowledging ownership (Luke 13:6)
     2. Relationship aware of expectancy (v. 6)
     3. Relationship anxious about disappointment (v. 7)
     4. Relationship appropriating nurture (v. 8)
     5. Relationship alert to justice (v. 9)

43

Selfishness

Luke 14:1-24

On entering the house of a notable Pharisee, Jesus was appalled by the display of selfishness on every hand. He spoke to the issue with great force because he knew that "whosoever exalteth himself shall be abased" (v. 11).

I. Selfishness defined
   "The exclusive consideration by a person of his own interest and happiness" (Webster).
   A. Selfishness is not a healthy "love of self"
   B. Selfishness is not a normal instinct of "self-preservation"
   C. Selfishness is a deifying of yourself
      1. Demonstrated by disobedience to God
      2. Demonstrated by disregard of people

II. Selfishness displayed
   A. Using people for the sake of an idea (v. 2)

    B. Abandoning principle for the sake of
       advantage (v. 5)
    C. Degrading others by upgrading yourself (v. 7)
    D. Assuming personal right to recognition (v. 7)
    E. Evaluating others by individual criteria (v. 8)
    F. Ministering for ulterior motives (v. 12)
    G. Reneging on commitments (v. 18)
    H. Hiding of reasons by excuses (v. 18)

III. Selfishness defeated
    A. The necessity of selfishness being defeated
       1. Selfishness leads to embarrassment (vv. 4,
          6, 9)
       2. Selfishness leads to abasement (v. 11)
       3. Selfishness leads to judgment (v. 14)
       4. Selfishness leads to impoverishment (v. 24)
    B. The possibility of selfishness being defeated
       1. By seeing selfishness for what it is
       2. By seeking deliverance with all your heart
       3. By submitting to lordship of Christ in
         obedience
       4. By sacrificing your lifestyle for others
       5. By securing the enabling of the Holy Spirit

44

Lostness

Luke 15:1-32

Jesus was constantly criticized for his association with people of questionable reputation. He explained that these people were "lost" and that it was a major part of his ministry to "seek" these lost people. He also made it clear that those who have no concern for the lost have little knowledge of God.

I. The condition of "lostness"
   Note: Greek, *apollumi*
   A. Lostness means destruction (Luke 4:34)
   B. Lostness means disintegration (5:37)
   C. Lostness means dissipation (9:24)
   D. Lostness means disorientation (15:4)

II. The causes of "lostness"
   A. Lostness through inevitable circumstances—"coins"
      1. Unaware of lostness
      2. Unable to act

B. Lostness through inherent character—"sheep"
   1. Aware of lostness
   2. Limited in ability
C. Lostness through individual choice—"son"
   1. Aware of lostness
   2. Able to act

III. The cure of "lostness"
  A. The divine side of the cure
    1. God who takes the initiative
      a. Personally (v. 6)
      b. Persistently (v. 8)
    2. Believers who share the burden
      Compare Pharisees and scribes (v. 2); elder
      brother (vv. 25–32)
  B. The human side of the cure
    1. Willingness to recognize (v. 17)
    2. Readiness to repent (v. 21)
    3. Openness to receive (vv. 22–24)

45

Astuteness

Luke 16:1-13

G ood men often do good things badly. Bad men sometimes do bad things well. In the parable of the unjust
steward, Jesus was not at all reluctant to use the steward
as an example of astuteness to his disciples.

I. Startling commendation of the unjust steward
   A. Commended by the lord not the Lord (v. 8)
   B. Commended for his "wisdom" not his injustice
      (v. 8)
      1. Its meaning
         a. Wisely (Gk.) *phronimōs*—"diaphragm;
            seat of intellect"
         b. For example, Genesis 3:1; Job 5:13;
            Ezekiel 28:4; Matthew 10:16
         c. Compare Luke 11:40; 12:20
      2. Its manifestation
         a. Astute enough to recognize his
            situation (Luke 16:3)

     b. Astute enough to resolve to act (v. 4)

     c. Astute enough to realize his assets (v. 5)

     d. Astute enough to react with alacrity (vv. 6–7)

II. Sweeping comments about unimpressive disciples Not astute enough in their comparison of

   A. Children of world and children of light (v. 8)

     1. Too slow to act

     2. Too slack in responsibility

     3. Too small in vision

     4. Too selfish in lifestyle

   B. That which is least and that which is much (v. 10)

     1. Attitude to "the least"–the secular

     2. Attention to "the much"–the spiritual

   C. That which is another's and that which is your own (v. 12)

     1. Earthly stewardship (another's)

     2. Heavenly riches (your own)

   D. God and mammon (v. 13)

     1. Serving God means mammon serves you

     2. Serving mammon means God serves you

     3. Serving both is an impossibility

III. Straightforward commands about unrighteous mammon

Note: *Mammon* (Aram.)–"wealth of every kind"

   A. Be astute in your handling of mammon because

     1. Mammon is a factor of stewardship (v. 11)

     2. Mammon is an indicator of faithfulness (v. 10)

     3. Mammon is a barometer of priorities (v. 9)

   B. Be aware of your own master (v. 13)

46

Worthiness

Luke 16:14-31

When Jesus said, "You cannot serve God and mammon," the money lovers in the group howled with laughter. They not only rejected what he said, but they also regarded him worthy of their derision. Jesus responded by explaining some home truths about true worthiness.

I. The worthiness that is projected by external factors
   Note: "Justify yourself before men" (v. 15)
   A. The factors
      1. Self-centered arrogance–"justify yourselves" (v. 15)
      2. Societal acclaim–"highly esteemed among men" (v. 15)
      3. Secular affluence–"fared sumptuously" (v. 19)
   B. The flaws
      1. Independence of divine law (v. 18)

    2. Indifference to lasting considerations (vv. 19–31)
    3. Indolence in spiritual concerns (v. 29)
    4. Intransigence in personal attitudes (vv. 27, 30)

II. The worthiness that is produced by internal factors
    Note: "God knoweth the hearts" (v. 15)
    A. The teaching of the law until John (v. 16)
       1. Announced by the Father (Deut. 5:6)
       2. Applied by the prophets (Deut. 5:33)
       3. Acted on by the people
          a. The warm hearts that responded
          b. The cold hearts that reacted
          c. The wicked hearts that perverted
    B. The preaching of the kingdom by Jesus (Luke 16:16)
       1. Born again to enter it (John 3:3, 5)
       2. Humble yourself to inherit it (Matt. 18:3–4)
       3. Move yourself to experience it (Luke 16:16)

III. The worthiness that is proved by eternal factors
    A. The eternity factor
       1. After the rich man's death and burial– Hades
       2. After the poor man's death–Abraham's bosom
    B. The responsibility factor
       1. Eternal destiny related to earthly considerations
       2. Eternal destiny related to response to truth (v. 31)
    C. The finality factor
       Note: "great gulf fixed" (v. 26)
    D. The reality factor
       1. The acclaimed may be disclaimed
       2. The despised may be exalted

47

The Bread of Life

John 6:25-71

When Christ was living among men, he was always the center of controversy. The centuries since have seen no real change. The reason is that his claims and challenges are so extraordinary that they demand reaction. But when taken seriously, they lead to life abundant.

I. The sign (John 6:1-15)
   A. An example of human need
   B. An act of compassion
   C. A miracle of significance (see John 20:30-31)

II. The significance
   Jesus is the bread of life (John 6:35, 41, 48, 51)
   A. The source of satisfaction
     1. Physical hunger met by loaves and fishes
     2. Spiritual hunger met by Christ
       a. Hunger for meaning
       b. Hunger for peace
       c. Hunger for contentment

3. Spiritual satisfaction requires coming to Christ
   a. Never hunger never thirst (v. 35)
   b. Coming to Christ related to divine initiative (v. 37)
   c. Coming to Christ impossible without the Father (v. 43)
   d. Going to Christ result of listening and learning (v. 45)
B. The source of security
   1. The awful inevitability of death (v. 49)
   2. The wonderful certainty of eternal life
      a. Life perishes, eternal life abides (v. 27)
      b. Eternal life is a gift (v. 27)
      c. The gift is received through faith (vv. 28–29, 47)
      d. The resurrection at the last day (v. 39)
      e. The assurance of being kept (v. 39)
   3. The basis of life is Christ's death
      a. The bread is my flesh which I give (v. 51)
      b. Man is lifeless without eating, drinking of Christ (v. 53)

III. The struggle
   A. The struggle to get significance across (v. 26)
   B. The struggle to promote seriousness (v. 27)
   C. The struggle against superficiality (v. 34)
   D. The struggle with self-sufficiency (vv. 60, 63)

48

The Light of the World

John 9:1-41

Blind beggars were not uncommon in Christ's time. When he met one and healed him on the Sabbath, he stirred up a great controversy. But when he claimed to be the light of the world, the challenge was firmly laid down.

I. The situation: Jesus meets a blind man
   A. The man's condition (v. 1)
      1. Congenital blindness
      2. Social deprivation
   B. The disciples' concern (vv. 2-3)
      1. What caused the problem
      2. Christ's answer
   C. The Savior's compassion
      1. Leading him—to be light (v. 5)
      2. Give sight—work of God (v. 4)
      3. To do right—making clay on Sabbath (v. 6)
      4. To make bright

     a. By taking initiative
     b. By challenging faith
     c. By requiring obedience
     d. By opening understanding
       (1) Man called Jesus (v. 11)
       (2) A prophet (v. 17)
       (3) A man from God (v. 33)
       (4) Lord—worship (v. 38)
       (5) Disciple (v. 27)

II. The clarification: I am the Light of the World
    A. The human condition
      1. Available light rejected (1:4–5, 9; 3:19–21)
      2. Unbelief compounded (12:37)
      3. Divine judgment enacted (12:39–40)
      4. The god of this world exacerbated (2 Cor. 4:4)
    B. The divine response
      1. To "let there be light"
      2. To ensure darkness does not triumph (John 1:5)
      3. To expose falsehood and promote truth (8:12)
      4. To offer direction and security (8:12)

III. The application: "You are the light of the world" (Matt. 5:14)
    A. Those who believe
    B. Those who behave

49

The Door of the Sheep

John 10:1-10

After the blind man had been thrown out of the synagogue (see 9:34), Jesus received him and in so doing set his authority over against that of the religious leaders. In case they missed the point, he added that he was the Door—and the only one at that!

I. The entrance to the kingdom
   Note: Shepherd/King/Ruler (Rev. 2:27; Matt. 2:6; Isa. 40:10–11)
   A. Shepherds' entrance
      1. God is the shepherd (Ps. 80:1; 23:1)
      2. He appoints undershepherds (Ezek. 34:1–2)
      3. They must enter through Christ (John 10:2)
      4. The tragedy of unfaithful shepherds (Ezek. 34:17–19)
   B. Sheep entrance
      1. An inclusive entrance—"whoever enters" (John 10:9)

2. An exclusive entrance—one Door to sheepfold (cf. 14:6)

II. The enemies of the kingdom
   A. They reject the exclusiveness of Christ (e.g., 1:10–11; 6:66)
   B. They resent the inclusiveness of salvation (e.g., 9:34)
      1. "You were steeped in sin at birth" (9:34)
      2. "How dare you lecture us!"
   C. They ruin the well-being of people
      1. They are thieves and robbers (10:8)
      2. They steal, kill, and destroy (v. 10)

III. The enjoyment of the kingdom
   Compare the bitter experience of the blind man
   A. The enjoyment of closeness of relationship
      1. Known by name (v. 3)
      2. Recognize his voice (v. 3)
   B. The enjoyment of fullness of grace (v. 10)
      1. Where sin abounds, grace hyper-abounds (Rom. 5:20)
      2. Where need exists, grace abounds (2 Cor. 9:8)
   C. The enjoyment of sureness of status
      1. Sure they have been received (John 10:9)
      2. Sure they are being led (vv. 4–5)
   D. The enjoyment of wholeness of life (v. 9)
      1. Saved—safe, healed
      2. Going in and out
      3. Finding pasture

50

The Good Shepherd

John 10:11-30

Christ's claim to be the Good Shepherd has been a source of comfort and assurance to believers down through the centuries. But when the claim was made, some of his hearers were so incensed that they tried to kill him, once again showing the challenging and controversial nature of his claims.

I. The unique character of the Good Shepherd
   A. I am the Shepherd
   B. I am the Shepherd, the Good (Gk. *kalos*)
      1. Caring deeply about the sheep (vv. 12–13)
      2. Giving totally for the sheep (vv. 11, 15, 17)

II. The unique claims of the Good Shepherd
    Claims about
    A. His sheep
       1. He knows them (v. 14)
       2. They know him (v. 14)

      3. They hear his voice (v. 27)
      4. They follow him (v. 27)
  B. His sheep pen
      1. I have other sheep (v. 16)
      2. I must bring them
      3. One flock, one Shepherd–Jews/Gentiles
  C. His signs (v. 25)
      1. Done in Father's name
      2. Done to validate his claims
  D. His sacrifice
      1. A voluntary sacrifice (v. 18)
      2. A vicarious sacrifice–"for the sheep" *(v. 15)*
      3. A victorious sacrifice (v. 17)
  E. His sonship
      1. Intimacy of relationship (v. 15)
      2. Authority for action (v. 18)
      3. Unity of purpose (v. 30)

III. The unique capabilities of the Good Shepherd
  A. To provide eternal life (v. 28)
  B. To preserve from perishing
  C. To protect from snatchers (v. 29)

51

The Resurrection and the Life

John 11:17-44

Jesus had proved his remarkable ability to heal, and many apparently accepted this without question (see vv. 21, 32, 37). But he wished to show his ability to conquer death as well as disease. So he raised Lazarus.

I. An illustration of human misery
   A. Discord—they tried to stone you (v. 8)
   B. Danger—we may die with him (v. 16)
   C. Death—already in the tomb (v. 17)
   D. Doubt—if you had been here (vv. 21, 32)
   E. Despair—going to mourn (v. 31)
   F. Disbelief—everyone will believe (v. 48)

II. A demonstration of divine majesty
   A. A majestic commitment (vv. 23-24)—"Your brother will rise again"
      1. Death is not final
      2. There is life after death

3. The dead will be raised (see John 5:28–29)
4. There is a final judgment
5. There are eternal options
B. A majestic claim (vv. 25–26)
   1. "I am the resurrection"
      a. I will conquer death
      b. I will preside over eternity
   2. "I am the life"
      a. Believers enjoy my life even in death
      b. Believers alive at my coming will never die
C. A majestic challenge (v. 26)–"Do you believe this?"
   1. I believe in the resurrection (v. 24)
   2. I have believed that . . .
   3. Roll away the stone (v. 39)
D. A majestic command (v. 43)–"Lazarus come out"
   1. Commands need to be obeyed
   2. The dead need power to obey
   3. Christ's command to have power within them

III. An application to contemporary ministry
   A. There's a life to be lived
   B. There's a death to be approached
   C. There's a judgment to confront
   D. There's a grace to be appropriated

52

The Way, the Truth, and the Life

John 13:31–14:14

The opposition to Jesus intensified after the raising of Lazarus, so he withdrew to a small village with his disciples. His public ministry was practically completed, but he had many things to tell the disciples, including word of his imminent departure.

I. Words of comfort for the troubled (13:31–14:4)
  A. Troubling words about
    1. Death (vv. 31–32; see 12:23–27)
      a. The Son of man glorified
      b. The glory of God demonstrated
      c. The plan of God fulfilled (12:27)
    2. Departure (13:33; see 8:21)
      a. Contemplating suicide?
      b. Deserting disciples who had left all for him?
      c. Disciples could follow later?
    3. Discipleship (13:34–35)
      a. The command to love

        b. The example of love
        c. The necessity for love
    4. Denial (vv. 36–38)
        a. Peter's noble intentions
        b. Peter's feeble performance
  B. Comforting words about
    1. Provision–"many rooms" *(14:2)*
    2. Preparation–"I am going to prepare for you" *(v. 2)*
    3. Promise–"I will come back" *(v. 3)*
    4. Prospects–"you may be where I am" *(v. 3)*
  C. Commanding words about
    1. Attitudes–"do not let" *(v. 1)*
    2. Faith–"Trust in God" *(v. 1)*

 II. Words of clarification for the confused
    Note: Thomas's response (v. 5)
  A. I am the way
    1. Into God's presence–(see Heb. 10:20)
    2. Into God's residence
  B. I am the truth
    1. Truth the basis of reality (see 14:6)
    2. Truth the grounds of certainty
  C. I am the life
    1. What is life?–*I am!*
    2. What is eternal life?–*I am!*
    3. What is spiritual life?–*I am!*

III. Words of challenge for the comforted
  A. If Christ is the way, what does this say about mission?
  B. If Christ is the truth, what does this say about belief?
  C. If Christ is the life, what does this say about heaven?

53

The True Vine

John 15:1-17

Both ancient and modern Israel have seen great symbolic significance in the vine and its fruit. The prophets and psalmists used it repeatedly, so Jesus' claim to be "the true vine" struck a responsive chord in the disciples. But what does it mean to us?

I. Christ is the vine
  A. Israel as the vine (Ps. 80)
    1. Planted (v. 8)
    2. Pampered (v. 9)
    3. Productive (vv. 10–11)
    4. Plundered (vv. 12, 13, 16)
    5. Plaintive (vv. 14–15, 17–19)
  B. Christ as the true vine
    1. A challenge to Israel's corruption
    2. A contrast to Israel's failure
    3. An answer to Israel's prayer
    4. The fulfillment of the Father's plan

II. The Father is the gardener
    A. He cares for the vine (John 15:10)
    B. He cuts out the dead wood (v. 2)
    C. He cleans the branches (v. 2)
        1. Already clean through the Word (v. 3)
        2. Process needs to be continual

III. The disciples are the branches
    A. The vine exists to bear fruit (see Ezek. 15)
       Note: No fruit–fruit–more fruit–much fruit
        1. Fruit–external evidence (Matt. 3:8)
        2. Fruit–practical performance (Gal. 5:22–23)
    B. The branches exist as a means to this end
        1. This is not optional
           a. You are the branches (John 15:5)
           b. You were chosen for this purpose (v. 16)
        2. This is not casual
           a. Pruning for the productive
           b. Unacceptability of the unfruitful
        3. This is not accidental
           a. Independence leads to barrenness (v. 4)
           b. Dependence is the key to fruitfulness (v. 7)
              (1) Dependence involves personal relationship–"In Me"
              (2) Dependence involves practical obedience–"My words"
              (3) Dependence involves prayerful contact–"Ask whatever"
        4. This is not temporal
           a. This kind of fruit lasts (v. 16)
           b. This fruit glorifies God (v. 8)

54

The Alpha and the Omega

Revelation 1:8-20

Alpha and *omega* are the first and last letters of the Greek alphabet. We use the expression "from A to Z" in different ways, but usually the meaning has to do with completeness and thoroughness. What did Jesus mean?

I. The meaning of the "I am" statements
   A. More than an announcement of arrival (John 6:20)
      1. A statement of authority
      2. A solution to fear
   B. More than a clarification of identity (John 8:23–30)
      1. A statement of equality (v. 29)
      2. An invitation to faith (v. 30)
   C. More than an assistance in a search (John 18:5–6)
      1. A statement of majesty
      2. A cause of humiliation

    D. More than a response to interrogation (Mark
       14:61–65)
       1. A statement of deity
       2. A charge of blasphemy
    E. More than an error of grammar (John 8:58–59)
       1. A statement of eternity
       2. A threat of death
          Note: See Exodus 3:14; Isaiah 41:4; 43:10;
          46:4

  II. The meaning of the "I am Alpha" statement
    A. The Alpha is the "Beginning"–Greek, *archē*
      (Rev. 21:6)
       1. The beginning of creation (Rev. 3:14)
       2. The first cause of creation
       3. The ruler of creation
    B. The Alpha is the "First"–Greek, *prōtos* (Rev.
      22:13)
       1. The First is the preeminent one
       2. The First accepts no second place (see Isa.
         44:6)

 III. The meaning of the "Omega" statement
    A. The Omega is "the End"–Greek, *telos*
       1. The End is the goal, objective (1 Peter 1:9)
       2. The End is the perfecter, finisher
       3. The End is the terminator (1 Peter 4:7, 17)
    B. The Omega is "the Last"–Greek, *eschatos*
       1. He has the last word
       2. There is no appeal after him

Part 5

Getting Ready for Christmas

55

Experiencing Life to the Full

John 10:10

In the midst of Christmas activity it is appropriate that we spend some time in reflection and contemplation on what lies behind the celebration. Among other things, Christ said he came that we might have life to the full.

I. Life and meaning
   "Modern man is experiencing a shortage of time and a shortage of meaning" (David Zach, *Futurist*)
   A. Modern man's dissatisfaction with dissatisfaction
      1. A longing for belonging–resenting loneliness
      2. A sense of significance–resenting abuse
      3. An expectation of fullness–resenting deprivation

B. Modern man's quest for meaning
  1. Who am I?–a search for identity
    a. A number?
    b. A naked ape?
  2. Why am I?–a search for meaning
    a. An accident?
    b. A coincidence?
  3. Where am I?–a search for integration
    a. Do I belong?
    b. Do I matter?
C. Modern man's suggested solutions
  1. Nihilism–God is dead; life is absurd
    a. Is God dead in our city?
    b. Do nihilists like being called absurd?
  2. Humanism
    a. No objective values; man may attach values
    b. Objective values exist; brute facts; discovered by intuition
  3. Christian theism
    Christ came to reveal objective meaning, significance

II. Life and success
  A. Success–"the achieving of a goal"
  B. Goal must be "worthwhile"
  C. Evaluated subjectively, objectively, collectively
  D. Be a successful person
    P–physically
    E–emotionally
    R–relationally
    S–spiritually
    O–occupationally
    N–nouthetically
      –Christ's incarnation
      –Christ's personality

-Christ's love
-Christ's life
-Christ's objective
-Christ's truth

III. Life and hope
Do we have a future?
A. I lay down my life
B. I take it up again

56

Recognizing the Truth

John 18:28-40

When Jesus stood before Pontius Pilate, he told him that he "came into the world, to testify to the truth." Pilate's response was, "What is truth?" But he didn't wait for an answer. Let's make sure we do.

    I. Truth and confusion
       A. The causes of confusion
          1. The father of lies (John 8:44)
          2. The family of lies
             a. Resisters of truth (Rom. 1:18)
             b. Perverters of truth (Rom. 1:25)
       B. The characteristics of confusion
          1. Confusion about deity (Gen. 2:1–4)
          2. Confusion about humanity (Gen. 3:5–6)
          3. Confusion about reality (Gen. 3:7–9)

   II. Truth and conviction
      "Everyone on the side of truth listens to me" (John 18:37)

    A. Listen to me about deity
        1. You're right, I am a king (v. 37)
        2. My kingdom is from another place (v. 36)
        3. "I came into the world" (v. 37)
    B. Listen to me about humanity
        1. "Men loved darkness instead of light" (3:19–20)
        2. "Whoever lives by the truth comes into the light" (3:21)
        3. "What he has done has been done through God" (3:21)
    C. Listen to me about reality
        1. "If I glorify myself, my glory means nothing" (8:54)
        2. "My Father . . . is the one who glorifies me" (8:54)

III. Truth and consequences
    A. Truth–something you believe
        1. An accurate statement demanding assent
        2. A reliable statement demanding commitment
    B. Truth–something you know
        1. Truth about bondage (8:34)
        2. Truth about liberty (8:32–36)
    C. Truth–something you do
        1. "Taught . . . the truth that is in Jesus" (Eph. 4:21)
        2. "No longer live as" (Eph. 4:17–32)
        3. "Put off" (Eph. 4:22–32)
        4. "Put on" (Eph. 4:24)

57

Seeking and Saving

Luke 5:27-32; 18:9-14; 19:1-10

Jesus stated that he had come to seek and save lost people and to call sinners to repentance. These statements produced both warm response and bitter reaction—and they still do.

I. The people to whom Christ came
   A. The "sinners" (5:32)
      1. The openly immoral (e.g., 18:11)
      2. Those with questionable occupations (e.g., tax collectors)
      3. Those who made empty professions of faith (Ps. 50:16–22; 49:6–15)
   B. The "lost" (Luke 19:10)
      1. A progressive state
         a. Lost—disorientation (cf. Luke 15)
         b. Perish—deterioration (cf. Luke 5:37)
         c. Destroy—disintegration (cf. Luke 17:27, 29)

      2. An ultimate condition
         Lost, perished, destroyed.
         Note: John 3:16; compare "eternal life"
   C. The "righteous" (Luke 5:32)
      1. The Pharisee in the temple (18:9–14)
      2. The prodigal's older brother (15:28–32)

II. The procedures Christ adopted
   A. He sat down with the sinners (19:5–10)
      1. By inviting himself
      2. By being welcomed
   B. He went after the "lost"
      1. Like a shepherd (15:4)
      2. Like a "master" (5:27)
   C. He spoke firmly to the "righteous"
      1. Go and learn (Hos. 6:6; Matt. 9:13)
      2. That means *hesed* rather than ritual

III. The purposes Christ accomplished
   A. Regeneration
   B. Repentance
   C. Restitution
   D. Rejoicing

58

The Sharp Edge of Christmas

Matthew 10:34-42

Christ's coming is usually seen in winsome, warm colors, and this is right and proper. But there is another side to the story—Christ promised that he would bring a sword and fire. What did he mean?

I. The incisive nature of discipleship
   A. The arena in which the disciple functions (v. 8)
      A world characterized by:
      1. Sickness
      2. Social ostracism
      3. Sorrow
      4. Spiritism
      5. Sin
   B. The authority which the disciple wields (v. 1)
      1. As a representative of the King
      2. As a proclaimer of the kingdom (v. 7)

C. The attitude which the disciple displays
   1. Refusal to be manipulated (vv. 9–15)
   2. Refusal to be intimidated (vv. 16–23)

II. The decisive nature of discipleship
   A. The decision to be content with the Master's lot (vv. 24–25)
      1. The abuse the Master suffered
      2. The disciple can expect the same
   B. The decision to confess the Master's name (vv. 32–33)
      1. The necessity of personal conviction
      2. The necessity of public confession
   C. The decision to consent to the Master's demands (vv. 37–39)
      1. He demands the supreme place (v. 37)
      2. He demands the supreme sacrifice (v. 38)
      3. He demands the supreme confidence (v. 39)

III. The divine nature of discipleship
   A. The disciple's commitment is divisive (vv. 34–36)
      1. Conflicting loyalties
      2. Conflicting lifestyles
   B. The disciple's communication is divisive (vv. 21–22)
      1. It is uncomplicated
      2. It is uncomplimentary
      3. It is uncompromising

59

Seeing the Light

John 12:37-50

The wise men saw the star and followed it to Bethlehem.
You could say they "saw the light." There were many
who also saw it but did not follow. Christ said, "I have
come into the world as a light," and he explained how
some respond and some don't–and why.

    I. Revelation–"I have come as a light"
        A. Life and light (John 1:4–9)
            1. In the beginning was the Word
            2. In him was life–inanimate, animate
            3. That life was the light of men
                a. Intelligence
                b. Moral sensitivity
                c. Spirituality
        B. Death and darkness
            1. Life and light sustained by loving
                obedience (Gen. 2:16–17)
            2. Death and darkness entered because of
                independent disobedience

3. Darkness
   a. Intelligence without faith
   b. Moral sensitivity without truth
   c. Spirituality without life
C. Light and darkness
   1. Believe or disbelieve (John 12:44)
   2. Trust or distrust (v. 36)
   3. Follow or wallow (8:12)

II. Reaction—"Who has believed?"
   A. Those who saw but would not believe (12:37)
      1. Saw signs without accepting significance
      2. Saw light but preferred darkness (3:19–21)
      3. Would not believe until they could not (12:39–40)
   B. Those who believed but would not confess (vv. 42–43)
      1. The perils of position, power, and prestige
      2. The prospect of judgment based on truth ignored (vv. 47–48)
   C. Those who believed and followed (see John 9)

III. Relevance—"You are the light of the world" (Matt. 5:14)
   A. Let your light shine
   B. Don't hide it
   C. Live for the Father's glory

60

Serving, Not Served

Matthew 20:20-28

Perhaps one of the most striking things Christ said about his incarnation was that he had not come to be served, but to serve, and that his disciples should develop the same attitude. Judging by the disciples' attitudes, this was not going to be easy.

I. An expression of self-interest
   A. The "self-interest" attitude
      1. "You only go around once"
         "If this is the situation . . . it is better not to" (Matt. 19:10)
      2. "You owe it to yourself"
         "What then will there be for us?" (19:27)
      3. "Staying ahead of the competition"
         "They began to grumble" (20:11)
      4. "Looking out for number one"
         The impertinence (v. 21) and the indignation (v. 24)

    B. The "self-interest" danger
       1. Ears deafened to the truth (vv. 17–19)
       2. Eyes blinded to the realities (v. 22)

II. An example of self-denial (v. 28)
    A. Self-designation—"Son of man"
       1. A messianic figure (Dan. 7:13–14)
       2. A frail human being (Ps. 8:4; see Heb. 2:5–9)
    B. Self-humiliation—"not to be served, but to serve"
       1. To be served—a divine right
       2. To serve—a divine decision
    C. Self-surrender—"give his life as a ransom"
       1. *Lytron*—price of a slave's freedom
       2. *Lytron*—deliverance for hostage, prisoner of war

III. An expectation of self-sacrifice (Matt. 20:26–27)
    Note: In pagan world, humility was a vice not a virtue
    A. To be great is to be *diakonos*
       1. The order of the towel
       2. The honor of the cross
    B. To be first is to be a *doulos*
    C. To be blest is to be a donor (Acts 20:35)
       1. The liberating effect of letting go
       2. The reciprocal result of generosity

Cassette tapes of the sermons preached from the outlines in this book are available from

TELLING THE TRUTH
P.O. Box 11
Brookfield, WI 53005

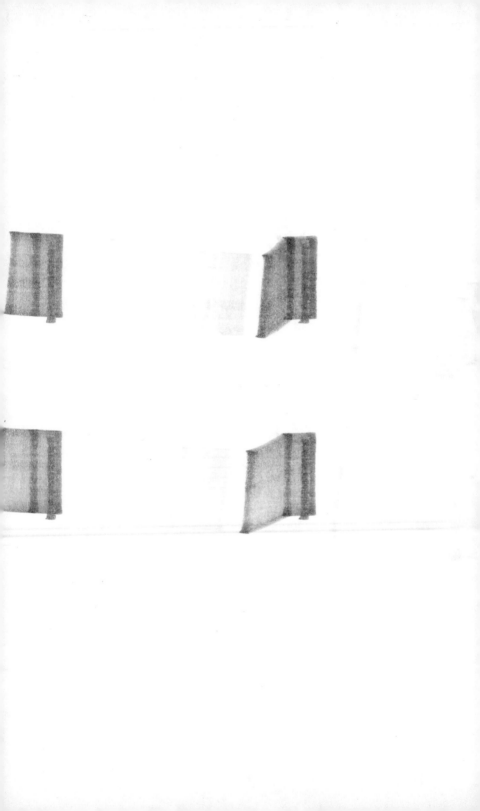